I want to be a
SERVICE STATION
ATTENDANT

By Eugene Baker

Illustrations by Richard Fickle

 CHILDRENS PRESS, CHICAGO

The author would like to thank Mr. Robert Jorgensen,
Midwest Regional Office, Gulf Oil Company, Park Ridge,
Illinois, for his assistance.

Library of Congress Catalog Card Number: 70-178495

Chuck sat in the front seat of the car. He was on a trip with his dad. Chuck enjoyed traveling. He followed the route on a map. They drove through small towns. Plain City . . . . Irwin . . . . Woodstock.

"Where are we now, Chuck?"
asked Dad.

Chuck had his finger on the map.
"Marysville is just ahead," he said.
"Look at the tall corn. This must
be good farmland."

Just then Dad started to slow
down the car. Bump—bump—bump!
"I think we are getting a flat tire,"
Dad said. "Let's pull off the highway.
I see a gas station ahead in
Marysville."

Very slowly, Dad turned the car into the gasoline service station. Bump—bump—bump went the tire. A young man walked toward them.

"Hello," he said with a smile. "May I help you?"

Chuck noticed that the service station attendant had his name—Jim—sewn onto his uniform.

"Yes, indeed," said Dad as he got out of the car. He walked around to the almost flat tire. Hisssssssss! Jim bent over it. He carefully ran his hand around the tire.

"It might have been a nail. Let me put on your spare tire. Then I will repair this one."

"Okay," said Dad. "I need gas and oil, too. Chuck, do you want to go across the street and have a hamburger?"

"If you don't mind, Dad, I'd like to stay here and watch Jim."

Jim smiled. "It's all right with me. We can talk while I work."

Dad nodded his head. "Fine. I'll see you both in a little while."

Jim soon had the spare tire out of the trunk of the car. Then he rolled a long narrow machine with a large handle under the car.

"This is our jack. If you want to help, Chuck, you can unscrew these nuts. They hold the tire in place," said Jim.

Soon the flat tire was off the car. Jim put on the spare tire. Then he began to repair the flat tire.

NX1912

"Jim, do you like working as a gas station attendant?" Chuck asked.

Jim looked up. "Yes, I do. I like helping people. Most customers seem happy when I can solve their car problems. Then they come back again to buy gas."

Chuck and Jim carefully put the repaired tire in the trunk.

"What exactly does an attendant do?" asked Chuck.

"You'll see. Come on, we'll service your dad's car. Then I will show you around the station."

Jim started the gas pump. He put the hose in the tank of the car. Chuck watched the meter on the gas pump. It showed how many gallons of gas were being pumped into the tank. It also showed how much money the gas would cost.

Jim opened the hood. He showed Chuck how to check the battery, the oil, the water, and the air in the other tires. Jim washed the windshield and the other windows. He also cleaned the rearview mirror and the headlights. He checked the windshield wipers.

Just then a lady drove into the station. She wanted directions to a nearby farm where strawberries were sold. Jim carefully explained how to get there, and waved good-bye. "That service is free," he laughed. "Come on inside, Chuck."

At the front of the station Jim said, "Here I handle cash payments. Sometimes I prepare a charge slip for a credit-card customer. I set up displays of oil and tires, and keep a count of these items. I provide highway maps and keep candy bars for hungry travelers."

Chuck followed Jim into the large service area. "Here is where we do repairs. We replace mufflers, rotate tires, change oil, and grease cars."

"What are these machines used for?" asked Chuck.

"This one helps me tune up a motor. This machine helps us balance the tires of a car."

Chuck picked up some tools from the bench. "I know what these are. You use pliers and screwdrivers and wrenches, too."

"Good for you," smiled Jim. "Let's have a bottle of pop before your dad gets back."

"One last question, Jim," said
Chuck as they stood out in front of
the station. "How did you become a
gas station attendant?"

"First I worked part time in a service station when I was in high school. I learned a lot from the station manager there. I don't mind working outside in all kinds of weather. I enjoy meeting people and I am good with machines. When I graduated from high school, this oil company sent me to its own training program. They taught me simple automobile repairs and sales. Someday I want to become a station manager."

Chuck's dad came across the street. "Ready to go, Sir!" called Jim.

"That's good work," said Dad, as he paid the bill.

Chuck picked up a new map and said, "Thanks for the map and the tour. When I'm older, I want to be a service station attendant, too."

Jim laughed. "That's great, Chuck!" Just then the station tow truck drove up. "Remember to learn how to drive. We provide emergency road service, too."

Dad and Chuck got into the car.
"I hope we don't need it," called Chuck
with a wave.

About the author:
Dr. Baker was graduated from Carthage College, Carthage, Illinois. He got his master's degree and doctorate in education at Northwestern University. He has worked as a teacher, as a principal, and as a director of curriculum and instruction. Now he works full time as a curriculum consultant. His practical help to schools where new programs are evolving is sparked with his boundless enthusiasm. He likes to see social studies and language arts taught with countless resources and many books to encourage students to think independently, creatively, and critically. The Bakers, who live in Arlington Heights, Illinois, have a son and two daughters.

About the Artist:
Richard Fickle lives with his wife, three children, three dogs and one cat in Wheaton, Illinois. One of his favorite aspects of illustration is the opportunity of informing others through his creative endeavors, just as he, himself, learns from each new assignment. Richard has many books and magazine illustrations to his credit, and considers his wife's encouragement one of the most important sources of his inspiration.